To:

From:

My favorite recipes are:

D1568681

TUNA BALLS

16 calories

1 can water packed tuna,
   drained & flaked
1-3 oz. pkg. Neufchatel
   cheese, softened
3 T. finely chopped celery

2 tsp. lemon juice
½ tsp. Worcestershire sauce
¼ tsp. salt
⅓ C. snipped parsley

Blend together tuna and cheese. Add celery, lemon juice, Worcestershire sauce, and salt and mix well. Shape into balls for appetizers. Roll in parsley. Chill well. Makes 30.

ONION PUFFS

¾ C. cream-style cottage
  cheese
1 tsp. instant minced onion
¼ tsp. salt
2 T. grated Parmesan cheese

1 T. finely chopped pimiento
2 drops hot pepper sauce
2 stiffly beaten egg whites
30 Melba toast rounds

Preheat oven to 450° F. Combine cottage cheese, onion and salt and beat with a rotary beater until smooth. Stir in cheese, pimiento, and hot sauce. Fold in egg whites. Spread mixture on toast rounds and bake at 450° F. for 8 to 10 minutes. Makes 30.

PICKLED MUSHROOMS

40 calories

16 large mushrooms, halved
¼ C. vinegar
2 T. soy sauce

1 tsp. salt
½ small onion, ringed

Place mushrooms in 1-quart jar. Heat remaining ingredients and pour into jar. Cover and refrigerate at least 24 hours before serving. Makes 4-½ cup servings.

PICKLED ARTICHOKES

30 calories

1-14 oz. can artichoke
  hearts, drained (reserve
  liquid)
2 T. minced onion

2 T. soy sauce
¼ C. vinegar
1 tsp. salt

Place artichoke hearts in 1-quart jar. Heat remaining ingredients to boiling and pour over artichoke hearts in jar. Cover and refrigerate 24 hours before using. Makes 4-½ cup servings.

PICKLED CUCUMBERS

15 calories

1 cucumber
1 small onion, sliced and
    separated
½ C. vinegar

½ C. water
¼ tsp. salt
Dash pepper

Run tines of fork lengthwise down cucumber to form grooves, slice. Combine cucumber and onion rings in bowl. Mix remaining ingredients and pour over cucumbers and onions. Cover and refrigerate 1 hour before draining and serving. Makes 4-½ cup servings.

WINE JELLY

10 calories per tablespoon.

1 C. wine
8 oz. sugar-free strawberry
  soda

1 T. sugar
1 env. unflavored gelatin
1 drop red food coloring

Combine wine, soda and sugar in saucepan. Sprinkle gelatin over liquid. Stir and cook over low heat until dissolved. Heat to boiling. Stir in food coloring. Pour into containers and cool. Cover and refrigerate. May be refrigerated up to 3 weeks. Makes 16 ounces.

BEVERAGES

FOAMING SODA   35 calories

For each serving: fill a tall glass ½ full with chilled sugar-free soda pop. Stir in 1½ tablespoons nonfat dry milk. Serve immediately.

STRAWBERRY FUZZ

50 calories

1-12 oz. can pineapple juice,
   chilled
1-10 oz. pkg. frozen
   strawberries, thawed

2-16 oz. bottles chilled
   lemon-lime beverage
Mint sprigs, optional

Combine pineapple juice, berries, ½ cup water in blender. Blend until fruit is pureed, strain. Pour mixture into a pitcher and slowly add carbonated lemon-lime beverage. Serve over ice. May be garnished with mint sprigs. Serves 10.

FRUIT COOLER

50 calories

1-6 oz. can frozen orange-
    grapefruit concentrate,
    thawed
2 C. cold water

Dash bitters
1¾ C. low-calorie lemon-lime
    beverage

Combine thawed concentrate, cold water and bitters. Chill. Just
before serving, add carbonated lemon-lime beverage. Serve over ice.
Serves 6.

EGGNOG

4 egg yolks
Noncaloric sweetener =
  ⅓ C. sugar
¼ tsp. salt
Nutmeg

1 tsp. vanilla
½ tsp. rum flavoring
4 egg whites
5 C. reconstituted nonfat dry
  milk

Beat egg yolks and sweetener together. Add salt and milk. Cook, stirring constantly until mixture begins to thicken. (Lightly covers metal spoon.) Add flavorings. Cool. Beat egg whites to soft peaks and fold cooked mixture into egg whites. Chill 4 hours. Sprinkle with nutmeg to serve if desired. Serves 14.

SOUPS

VEGETABLE SOUP
70 calories

3 C. pork broth
1-8 oz. can sauerkraut
1 bay leaf
1 tsp. salt
1 C. diced carrots

1 C. diced celery
2 tomatoes, peeled and cut in
   wedges
¼ to ⅓ C. barley
3 T. snipped parsley

Skim fat from pork broth. Cut up sauerkraut while still in can. Combine all ingredients except parsley and heat to boiling. Reduce heat, cover, and cook until carrots are tender. Remove bay leaf. Sprinkle with parsley to serve. Serves 6.

APPETIZER SOUP

1 ⅓ C. water
2 beef bouillon cubes
1 ½ tsp. horseradish

1 tsp. lemon juice
¼ tsp. dill weed
5 lemon slices

Heat all ingredients, except lemon, to boiling. Serve hot and garnish with lemon slices. Serves 5.

FRENCH ONION SOUP

42 calories

1 onion, thinly sliced
1 T. margarine
2 cans condensed beef broth
¾ C. water

¾ tsp. Worcestershire sauce
Dash pepper
1½ T. grated Parmesan cheese

Cook onion in margarine until lightly browned. Add beef broth, water, and Worcestershire sauce. Bring to a boil and season with pepper. Sprinkle with cheese to serve. Serves 6.

TARRAGON SOUP

2 T. butter or margarine
¼ C. minced onion
¼ C. minced celery
4 C. tomato juice
1 tsp. salt

¼ tsp. pepper
1 T. sugar
1 tsp. dried tarragon
Tabasco sauce

Saute onion and celery in butter until golden brown. Add tomato juice, salt, pepper, sugar, tarragon, and a few drops Tabasco; bring to a boil, reduce heat, simmer 5 minutes.

FISH CHOWDER

1 lb. halibut fillets
3 C. tomato juice
1 medium onion, chopped
2 lemon slices

1 bay leaf
½ tsp. salt
2 peppercorns
Parsley

Thaw fish. Cut fish into bite-size pieces. Combine all ingredients except fish and parsley and bring to a boil. Add fish and return to boiling. Reduce heat, cover, simmer 4 to 6 minutes. Sprinkle with parsley. Serves 5.

COTTAGE CHEESE DIP

2 T. milk
½ tsp. Worcestershire sauce
  or lemon juice

1-12 oz. carton cream-style
  cottage cheese
Dash of salt

Blend the above in a blender.
VARIATIONS: 1. Cheddar cheese; 2. Onion soup mix; 3. Tuna, 1
tablespoon capers, 1 teaspoon horseradish, ¼ teaspoon each: celery
and garlic salt, monosodium glutamate.

COOKED CHEESE DRESSING   22 calories per tablespoon.

2 T. flour
2 T. sugar
1 tsp. salt
1 1/4 tsp. prepared mustard

3/4 C. skim milk
2 slightly beaten egg yolks
2 T. lemon juice
2 T. vinegar

Combine flour, sugar, salt, and mustard in a saucepan and gradually stir in milk. Cook and stir over medium heat until thick and bubbly. Stir about 1/4 of mixture onto egg yolks and return to hot mixture. Cook and stir over low heat for 1 minute. Stir in lemon juice and vinegar and chill. Makes 1 cup.

BLUE CHEESE DRESSING

18 calories per tablespoon.

1 C. cream-style cottage
   cheese
⅓ C. water

2 T. blue cheese, crumbled
¾ tsp. Worcestershire sauce

Place all ingredients in blender and blend until smooth. Chill. Makes
1 cup.

COTTAGE-DILL DRESSING   16 calories per tablespoon.

1 C. cream-style cottage   2 T. chopped dill pickle
   cheese   1 T. minced onion
1 ½ T. lemon juice

Combine cottage cheese, lemon juice and ⅓ cup water in blender
and blend until smooth. Stir in pickle and onion. Chill. Makes 1 cup.

MOCK THOUSAND ISLAND DRESSING   25 calories/tablespoon

1-3 oz. pkg. Neufchatel
  cheese, softened
¼ C. chili sauce

¾ tsp. horseradish
2 T. chopped green pepper

Blend together cheese, chili sauce and horseradish until smooth. Stir in green pepper. Chill. Makes ⅔ cup.

MOCK MAYONNAISE

20 calories

1 C. unflavored yogurt
2 T. mayonnaise
¼ tsp. salt

1/8 tsp. paprika
1 drop yellow food coloring

Mix all ingredients until well mixed and smooth. Refrigerate 2 hours before serving. Makes 16-1 tablespoon servings.

CABBAGE-MEAT CASSEROLE

1 small head cabbage	Sweet basil
1 lb. ground beef	Garlic to taste
1 onion, chopped	¾ C. raw brown rice
Salt to taste	3 cans tomato soup
Pepper to taste	2¼ C. hot water
Celery seed to taste	1 C. sauerkraut, optional
Oregano to taste	

Preheat oven to 350° F. Cut cabbage into wedges. Pour hot water to cover and drain. Set aside. Brown beef with seasonings, put cabbage in bottom of casserole. Add layer of rice and meat mixture and sauerkraut. Add soup which has been diluted with 2¼ cups water. Cover and bake 1½ to 2 hours or until rice is done.

STUFFED PEPPERS

212 calories

8 green peppers
Salt
1 lb. lean ground beef
⅓ C. chopped onion
1½ C. croutons

1 C. shredded mozzarella
  cheese
2 tomatoes, chopped
½ tsp. Worcestershire sauce
½ tsp. salt

Preheat oven to 350° F. Cut off tops of green peppers and remove insides. Precook in boiling salt water for 5 minutes. Sprinkle insides with salt. Brown ground beef and onion and drain. Stir in croutons, ½ cup cheese, tomatoes, Worcestershire sauce and salt. Fill peppers. Place in shallow baking dish and cover. Bake at 350° F. for 25 minutes. Sprinkle with remaining cheese and bake, uncovered, 5 to 10 minutes more. Serves 8.

BEEF PATTIES

1 C. water	½ green pepper
1 medium carrot	½ stalk celery
1 medium onion	8 oz. ground beef

Place water, carrot, onion, pepper and celery in blender and chop. Drain well. Mix with ground beef and form 3 patties. Broil until browned.

BASIC MEAT LOAF

271 calories

1 beef bouillon cube
1 beaten egg
1 ⅓ C. soft bread crumbs
⅓ C. chopped onion

½ tsp. ground sage
1 lb. lean ground beef
3 T. chili sauce

Preheat oven to 350° F. Dissolve bouillon cube in ¼ cup boiling water. Mix bouillon, egg, crumbs, onion, sage, ¼ teaspoon salt and dash of pepper. Add beef and mix well. Shape into a loaf in shallow baking dish. Bake at 350° F. for 45 minutes. Top with chili sauce and bake 10 to 15 minutes more. Serves 4.

CABBAGE-HAMBURGER CASSEROLE

Wash 1/3 cup wild rice 4 to 5 times. Soak 7 to 8 hours before cooking. Cook rice for 20 minutes. Combine rice, 1 pound hamburger, browned, 1/4 cup onions, chopped and sauteed, 1 can each mushroom and celery soup, 1 can water, salt and pepper to taste, and heat. Slice 1 head cabbage. Layer cabbage and meat mixture in casserole beginning with cabbage. Bake 1 1/2 hours.

BURGERS 'N SPROUTS

190 calories

2 lbs. lean ground beef
½ C. bean sprouts, chopped
⅓ C. finely chopped water
   chestnuts

2 tsp. salt
2½ tsp. soy sauce

Mix all ingredients together. Shape into 8 patties. Broil patties 3" from heat about 5 minutes on each side. Serves 8.

TACOS

1 ½ lbs. lean ground beef
1 env. taco seasoning mix
½ tsp. salt
1 C. water
12 taco shells
¾ C. shredded Cheddar
  cheese

⅔ C. chopped tomato
⅔ C. shredded lettuce
⅔ C. onion
⅔ C. chopped cucumber
Taco sauce

Cook and stir ground beef until browned. Drain off all fat. Stir in taco seasoning, salt and water. Boil. Reduce heat and simmer 15 to 20 minutes. Heat taco shells. Spoon ¼ cup meat mixture into each shell and top with desired vegetables and taco sauce. Serves 12.

POT ROAST

1 beef pot roast	2 to 3 stalks celery, diced
1 tsp. salt	2 carrots, sliced
1/8 tsp. pepper	½ C. peas
½ tsp. ground ginger, opt.	1 whole tomato, quartered
1 clove garlic, minced	½ C. water
1 onion, sliced	¾ C. tomato juice

Combine salt, pepper and ginger and rub mixture into meat. Brown meat on all sides in a heated Dutch oven. Add remaining ingredients, except tomato, and cover tightly. Cook about 3 hours until meat is tender. Add tomato and cook 5 minutes more.

29

STUFFED CABBAGE ROLLS

240 calories

1 small head cabbage
1 lb. lean ground beef
1 medium onion, chopped
1-16 oz. can red kidney
  beans, drained
1 C. creamed cottage cheese

½ tsp. ground allspice
Salt
1-16 oz. can tomatoes
1 T. brown sugar
¼ C. water
2 tsp. cornstarch

Remove core and outside leaves of cabbage. Place cabbage in boiling water and remove 8 outside leaves as they soften. Coarsely shred

(cont.)

remaining cabbage. Cook ground beef and onion until beef is browned and onion is tender. Remove from heat and add kidney beans, cottage cheese and allspice and salt. Place about ½ cup mixture on each cabbage leaf. Fold 2 edges of leaf to center over meat. Starting at one narrow end roll leaf as for jellyroll. Place shredded cabbage in bottom of skillet used to brown ground beef and arrange stuffed cabbage leaves, seam-side down, on shredded cabbage. Add tomatoes, including liquid, brown sugar and ¾ teaspoon salt. Heat to boiling, stirring gently to break up tomatoes. Reduce heat and simmer 45 minutes or until cabbage is tender. Combine water and cornstarch and gradually add to cabbage mixture. Cook until mixture begins to thicken. Serves 8.

LASAGNA

¾ lb. lean ground beef
1 small onion, diced
1-28 oz. can tomatoes
1-6 oz. can tomato paste
½ C. water
2 tsp. brown sugar
1 ½ tsp. salt

1 tsp. oregano
½ tsp. garlic powder
¼ tsp. pepper
12 lasagna noodles
2 C. lowfat cottage cheese
1 egg
8 oz. part-skim mozzarella
cheese, grated

Cook ground beef and onion in Dutch oven until all pan juices evaporate and onion is tender. Stir frequently. Add tomatoes with

(cont.)

their liquid, tomato paste, water, brown sugar, salt, oregano, garlic powder and pepper. Heat to boiling. Reduce heat and simmer, covered, 30 minutes, stirring occasionally. Prepare lasagna noodles according to package directions. Press cottage cheese through sieve into a bowl and add egg. Preheat oven to 375°. Arrange half of noodles into a 9x13" pan. Spoon half of cottage cheese mixture over noodles; sprinkle with half of mozzarella and top with half of meat sauce; repeat. Bake 40 minutes or until heated through. Let stand 20 minutes. Serves 10.

BEEF AND SAUERKRAUT STEW

300 calories

2 slices bacon, diced
1 ½ lb. stew beef; 1" chunks
1 medium onion, diced
4 tsp. paprika
2 C. water

2 T. catsup
¾ tsp. salt
¼ tsp. pepper
2 C. drained sauerkraut
¼ tsp. caraway seeds

Brown bacon in Dutch oven over medium heat. Drain on paper towels. Cook beef and onion in bacon drippings until meat is lightly browned and onion is tender (15 minutes), stirring occasionally. Stir in paprika and cook 1 minute more. Stir in water, catsup, salt and pepper and heat to boiling. Reduce heat and simmer 1½ hours, stirring occasionally. Skim off fat. Add sauerkraut and caraway seeds and cover and simmer 30 minutes more. Sprinkle bacon over stew. Serves 6.

LIVER STRIPS

170 calories

1 lb. sliced liver, cut in 1"
   strips
1 tsp. beef bouillon

½ onion, sliced
½ C. tomato sauce

Coat skillet with vegetable spray-on and cook meat and bouillon until meat is brown. Stir in onion and tomato sauce. Reduce heat, cover and cook until meat is done. Serves 4.

CUBE STEAKS

250 calories

4 beef cube steaks
¼ C. low-calorie Italian
  dressing

1 medium tomato, cut in
  eighths
Salt

Place meat in skillet coated with vegetable spray-on. Pour dressing over meat and cover and let stand 20 minutes. Turn once. Brown meat about 4 minutes on each side. About 2 minutes before meat is desired doneness, add tomatoes. Season with salt. Serves 4.

ONION STEAK

1 ½ lb. round steak
¼ C. flour
2 T. shortening
2 onions, sliced

1 T. vinegar
½ clove garlic, minced
1 bay leaf
¼ tsp. crushed thyme

Trim excess fat from steak. Combine flour, 1 teaspoon salt and dash of pepper and dredge steak. Cut into 6 serving size pieces. Brown in hot shortening and drain. Top with onion slices and stir in 1 cup water and remaining ingredients. Bring to a boil and reduce heat. Cover and simmer 1 hour. Remove bay leaf to serve. Serves 6.

LEMON-PEPPER STEAK

1 T. grated lemon peel
1 T. butter or margarine,
  softened
2 tsp. cracked black pepper
1 tsp. salt

1 clove garlic, minced
1 top round steak, 1¼"
  thick (2 lb.)
Lemon slices
Parsley sprigs

Mix butter, lemon peel, pepper, salt and garlic together in a small bowl. Spread half of mixture on one side of beef steak and broil 8 minutes. Spread other side of steak with remaining mixture and broil other side to desired degree of doneness. Garnish with lemon slices and parsley to serve. Serves 8.

VEAL SPECIALTY

10 veal patties
Salt and pepper to taste
2 C. tomato juice
1 beef bouillon cube

1 tsp. Worcestershire sauce
1 tsp. oregano
¼ tsp. dry mustard
Onion flakes

Preheat oven to 350° F. Brown veal patties which have been salted and peppered. Blend tomato juice, beef bouillon, Worcestershire sauce, oregano, mustard, salt and pepper to taste. Simmer until bouillon cube is dissolved. Place veal patties in a 9x13" pan (they will overlap). Pour sauce over veal patties and top with onions. Bake, uncovered, 30 minutes.

FRENCH VEAL SAUTE

½ C. Burgundy wine
1 ½ lbs. lean stew veal
1 T. salad oil
½ C. canned mushrooms
¼ clove garlic

½ C. chopped onion
¼ C. chopped green pepper
1 C. tomatoes, peeled &
   chopped
½ C. diced green pepper

Saute meat in oil until light brown on all sides. Remove meat. Add garlic, onion, and mushrooms. Saute until onion is tender. Add green pepper, tomatoes, wine and meat. Cover and cook 1½ hours. Add water if necessary. Sprinkle with parsley if desired. Serves 4.

PORK CHOPS

6 pork chops
6 pineapple rings
½ C. pineapple juice
¼ tsp. brown sugar
   substitute

¼ tsp. cinnamon
Dash rosemary leaves
1 C. celery, diced
1 green pepper, cut into
   strips

Trim all fat from chops. Brown meat on all sides in skillet. Remove chops. Mix pineapple juice, sugar, cinnamon, and rosemary in skillet. Put chops in pan and sprinkle with salt and pepper, add celery and cover. Simmer about 30 minutes. Add green pepper strips and place pineapple rings on each chop. Cover and cook about 10 minutes more.

CURRIED PORK CHOPS

265 calories

4 pork chops, ½" thick
2 medium cooking apples
1 medium chopped onion
1 T. curry powder

¾ C. water
1¼ tsp. salt
¼ tsp. sugar

Trim fat from pork chops. Heat fat trimmings in skillet and press fat to leave about 1 tablespoon liquid. Discard fat pieces. In hot fat, cook pork chops until browned on both sides. Peel and grate 1 apple; core remaining apple and cut into 12 wedges. Cook onion in remaining

(cont.)

fat in skillet until tender. Stir in curry powder and cook 1 minute. Return pork chops to skillet and add water, salt, sugar and grated apple. Heat to boiling. Reduce heat; cover, and simmer 40 minutes or until chops are tender. Add apple wedges and heat through. Serves 4.

PORK CHOPS AND PINEAPPLE

300 calories

4 lean pork chops, ½" thick
1-8 oz. can sliced pineapple
   in unsweetened juice
   (reserve ¼ C. juice)
¼ C. soy sauce

¼ tsp. monosodium glutamate
¼ tsp. garlic powder
Paprika
Parsley

Trim chops. Place chops in ungreased 8x8" dish. Mix pineapple juice, soy sauce, monosodium glutamate and garlic powder together and pour over chops. Cover, and refrigerate about 8 hours. Turn once or twice. Heat oven to 350° F. Top each chop with a pineapple slice and sprinkle with paprika. Cover with foil and bake about 45 minutes. Uncover and bake 5 minutes longer. Garnish with parsley. Serves 4.

SUPPER SALAD

105 calories

1-16 oz. can sauerkraut,
   drained, reserve liquid
1 onion, sliced

2 dill pickles, cut into strips
1 tart apple, pared & cored
1⅓ C. cooked ham, diced

Layer ⅓ of each ingredients in bowl, repeat twice. Drizzle with sauerkraut juices. Cover and refrigerate 1¼ hours. Serves 4.

PORK ROLL

1 tsp. salt
½ tsp. ground allspice
½ tsp. pepper
½ tsp. sage
3 lb. rolled pork loin roast
6 whole cloves

4 C. water
2 C. diced celery
1 T. minced onion
2 bay leaves
6 peppercorns
6 whole allspice

Combine salt, ground allspice, pepper and sage and rub into meat. Insert cloves into meat. Place meat and remaining ingredients in a Dutch oven and heat to boiling. Reduce heat, cover, and simmer 1½ hours turning after ¾ hour. Remove from heat, cover meat with a plate and weight to press roast. When cool, remove meat from broth and remove string. Cut meat into ¼" slices. Makes 22 slices.

WIENER-KRAUT BAKE

210 calories

1-16 oz. can sauerkraut,
   drained and cut
$2/3$ C. vegetable juice
   cocktail
2 tsp. onion

1 T. mustard
4 frankfurters
1 green pepper, sliced in
   rings

Preheat oven to 350° F. Combine sauerkraut, vegetable juice, onion and mustard, and place in casserole. Place frankfurters on top of sauerkraut mixture. Bake, uncovered, at 350° F. for 50 minutes. Top with green pepper rings and bake another 10 minutes. Serves 4.

HAM AND SALAD ROLLS

207 calories

4 frankfurter buns, split
5 tsp. mustard
1 ¼ C. shredded lettuce
⅓ C. cucumber slices

2 T. low-calorie French
 dressing
8 slices boiled ham
4 dill pickle strips

Spread cut sides of buns with mustard. Mix lettuce, cucumber and dressing together. Place ¼ of mixture on one end of a stack of 2 ham slices and top with 1 pickle slice. Roll up as for jellyroll. Place in bun. Serves 4.

STEAMED CHICKEN

180 calories

1 lg. head chicory or
  escarole
4 medium carrots, cut into
  1/4" slices
1-2½ lb. broiler-fryer, cut-up

2 T. cooking or dry sherry
2 T. soy sauce
1/4 tsp. salt
1/4 tsp. ground ginger

Wash chicory and trim any rough or tough stems. Cut into 3" long
pieces. Place leaves in skillet and arrange carrot slices over the top
and top with chicken pieces. Combine sherry, soy sauce, ginger, and
salt and pour over chicken and vegetables. Heat mixture to boiling.
Reduce heat and simmer 45 minutes or until chicken is fork tender.
Serves 4.

CHICKEN CASSEROLE

2 whole chicken breasts
1-16 oz. can French-style
   green beans
1-8½ oz. can peas

½ lb. sliced mushrooms
1 C. water
2 chicken bouillon cubes
¼ C. soy sauce

Preheat oven to 350° F. Arrange chicken and vegetables in a baking dish. Dissolve bouillon in hot water, and blend in soy sauce. Pour over chicken and vegetables. Let stand a few minutes before baking. Bake for 30 minutes or until chicken is tender.

SOY-GLAZED CHICKEN

275 calories

1-20 oz. can sliced
   pineapple, in own juices
¼ C. soy sauce
1 tsp. instant minced onion

½ tsp. ground ginger
¼ tsp. garlic powder
2-2½ lb. broiler fryers,
   quartered

Preheat oven to 375° F. Drain pineapple and reserve ¼ cup juice. Mix pineapple juice, soy sauce, onion, ginger and garlic powder together in a roasting pan. Add chicken and coat well. Arrange chicken in roaster with skin side up. Bake 50 to 60 minutes or until chicken is fork-tender; basting with juices occasionally. Add pineapple and bake an additional 5 minutes. Serves 8.

CHICKEN WITH MUSHROOM GRAVY

230 calories

6 chicken breast halves
1 C. tomato juice
1-4 oz. can mushroom
  pieces, drained-reserve
  liquid
⅓ C. finely chopped onion

1 T. parsley flakes
1½ tsp. salt
1 tsp. basil leaves
1/8 tsp. garlic powder
2 tsp. cornstarch
2 T. water

Place skinned chicken in a heated skillet treated with vegetable spray-on. Brown chicken. Pour tomato juice and mushroom liquid over chicken. Stir in onion, parsley, salt, basil leaves and garlic powder. Cover and simmer about 60 minutes or until chicken is done. Stir in mushrooms. Mix cornstarch into water and stir into liquid in skillet. Cook, stirring constantly, until mixture thickens and boils. Boil and stir 1 minutes. Serves 6.

CHICKEN ORIENTAL

1 to 2 frying chickens,
   quartered & skinned
½ C. soy sauce
2 cloves garlic, minced
1 tsp. ginger

2 T. oil
½ tsp. salt
¼ tsp. pepper
1 T. sherry

Preheat oven to 350° F. Mix soy sauce, garlic, ginger, oil, salt, pepper and sherry. Pour over chicken. If time allows, marinate all day in refrigerator. Bake 1 hours and 30 minutes.

GREEN PEPPERS AND CHICKEN

190 calories

2½ to 3 lb. chicken, cut-up
and skinned
¼ C. soy sauce
1 T. water
½ tsp. garlic powder

1-8½ oz. can water chestnuts,
drained & sliced
1 green pepper, sliced
2 tsp. cornstarch
2 T. water

Place chicken in skillet. Mix soy sauce, 1 tablespoon water and garlic powder and pour over chicken. Cover and refrigerate 1 hour. Turn chicken after 30 minutes. Heat contents of skillet to boiling, reduce heat and simmer 40 minutes. Distribute green pepper slices and water chestnuts over chicken. Cover and simmer until chicken is tender. Combine cornstarch and water and stir into liquid in skillet. Cook and stir until mixture thickens and boils. Boil and stir 1 minute. Serves 6.

OPEN-FACE CHICKEN SANDWICHES

139 calories

DRESSING:
2 T. flour
1 T. sugar
1 ¼ tsp. dry mustard
½ tsp. salt
Dash cayenne
2 slightly beaten egg yolks
¾ C. skim milk
3 T. vinegar

SANDWICHES:
1-5 oz. can water chestnuts,
   drained and sliced
Paprika
8 slices whole wheat bread
32 sprigs watercress
8 slices cooked chicken

Combine first 5 ingredients and mix well. Stir in egg yolks and milk. Cook and stir over low heat until thick and bubbly. Stir in vinegar and chill. Roll edges of half of the water chestnut slices in paprika and set aside. Spread bread with dressing and top each slice with 4 sprigs watercress, 1 slice chicken, some of remaining water chestnut slices. Top with few slices paprika edged water chestnuts. Serve with remaining dressing. Serves 8.

55

OVEN BAKED CHICKEN

BASTING SAUCE:
1 tsp. garlic salt
1 tsp. curry powder
¼ C. boiling water

1 chicken bouillon cube
1 tsp. Worcestershire sauce
½ tsp. oregano
¼ tsp. paprika

Preheat oven to 350° F. Salt chicken and place in shallow baking dish. Combine ingredients for sauce. Brush both sides of chicken with sauce and pour remaining sauce over chicken. Bake 50 to 60 minutes. Chicken may be turned during baking but is not necessary. Chicken may be marinated in sauce for several hours before baking.

TUNA SALAD SANDWICHES

157 calories

1 can water-packed tuna, drained
¼ C. cream-style cottage cheese
¼ C. chopped celery
1½ T. chopped sweet pickle
1 T. minced onion
1 T. low-calorie mayonnaise
¼ tsp. salt
4 slices whole wheat bread
4 tsp. low-calorie mayonnaise
4 lettuce leaves
4 slices tomato
Salt

Combine first 7 ingredients. Set aside. Spread each slice of bread with 1 teaspoon mayonnaise. Top with lettuce leaf, tomato slice, and a few grains of salt. Spread ¼ of tuna mixture on top of each tomato slice. Serves 4.

TURKEY ROLL

2 to 2½ lb. turkey roast
½ C. rose
1 T. soy sauce

½ tsp. rosemary leaves
½ tsp. marjoram leaves

Mix all ingredients except roast and pour over roast in baking dish. Cut roast into ½" slices and spoon pan juices over each slice. Serves 10.

POACHED RED SNAPPER

2 C. water
1 lemon, sliced
1 small onion
3 peppercorns

2 sprigs parsley
1 bay leaf
4-6 oz. portions red snapper,
  skinned & boned

Combine all ingredients, cover, and simmer 6 to 8 minutes or until fish is tender.

SALMON IN FOIL

2 T. diet margarine
1 T. mayonnaise
1 T. lemon juice
¼ tsp. salt

¼ tsp. paprika
¼ tsp. dill weed
16 oz. can salmon
⅔ C. celery

Preheat oven to 350° F. Heat margarine in custard cup set in hot water. Remove from heat and beat in mayonnaise, lemon juice, salt, paprika, and dill. Place salmon and celery in center of foil and add margarine mixture on top of salmon. Fold foil together and bake 20 to 30 minutes. Serves 2.

FISH DINNER

1-16 oz. pkg. frozen haddock
  or cod fillets
1 large cucumber
1 medium lemon, sliced
1-2 oz. jar pimento, drained
  cut into strips

½ tsp. salt
¼ tsp. instant chicken
  bouillon
1/8 tsp. pepper
1/8 tsp. Italian seasoning

Preheat oven to 450° F. Remove frozen fish from freezer and let thaw at room temperature for 15 minutes. Cut cucumber lengthwise, remove seeds, cut to ¼" thick slices. Cut frozen fish to 4 equal portions. Wrap ¼ each fish, cucumber, lemon and remaining ingredients in foil. Seal well. Place foil packets in a 9x13" pan, seam side up. Bake 30 to 35 minutes. Serves 4.

TANGY FISH

1 lb. fish fillets
1 C. tomato juice
¼ C. mustard

1 T. instant minced onion
1/8 tsp. pepper

Preheat oven to 350° F. Place fish in casserole. Mix together all other ingredients and pour over fish. Bake 20 to 30 minutes, or until fish is done.

FISH STICKS

1-16 oz. pkg. frozen pike or
  flounder fillets, skinless
1 tsp. salt
½ tsp. dill weed
2 drops red pepper sauce

⅓ C. unsweetened grapefruit
  juice
¾ tsp. paprika
1 T. minced onion
6 lengthwise slices dill pickle
Parsley

Cut fish into 6 sticks. Arrange in ungreased baking dish. Combine salt, dill weed, red pepper sauce and grapefruit juice and pour over fish. Let stand at room temperature for 1 hour, turning fish frequently. Heat oven to 475° F. Sprinkle fish with paprika and top each fish stick with onion and dill pickle slice. Bake, uncovered, about 15 minutes. Garnish with parsley. Serves 3.

POACHED FISH WITH VEGETABLES

225 calories

1-16 oz. pkg. frozen flounder
  sole or perch fillets
2 T. salad oil
3 medium carrots, cut into
  thin strips
1 green pepper, diced
1 medium onion, diced

1 garlic clove, minced
¾ tsp. salt
½ tsp. basil
1-16 oz. can tomatoes
2 T. water
2 tsp. cornstarch
1 sliced lemon

Let frozen fish fillets thaw at room temperature for about 15 minutes. Heat salad oil and cook carrots, green pepper, onion, garlic, salt and basil until tender and crisp, stirring frequently. Add tomatoes with liquid, stirring to break up. Cut fillets crosswise into 8 pieces. Add fish to vegetable mixture and heat to boiling. Reduce heat, cover, and simmer 5 to 10 minutes. Stir water and cornstarch together and stir into liquid in skillet. Cook until mixture thickens and boils, stirring gently, boil 1 minute. Garnish with lemon slices. Serves 4.

TURBOT ITALIANO

1 lb. turbot
¼ C. tomato sauce

1 tsp. dry spaghetti sauce mix
OR garlic salt and pinch of
oregano

Preheat oven to 350° F. Bake turbot about 30 minutes. Put sauce over fish and bake another 10 minutes. Sprinkle with spaghetti sauce mix and top with grated mozzarella cheese. Return to oven just until cheese melts.

ORANGE HALIBUT FILLETS

142 calories

1 lb. halibut fillets
2 T. orange juice
 concentrate
1 T. snipped parsley

1 T. juice
½ tsp. dried dill weed
4 thin orange slices
¼ tsp. salt

Cut fish into 4 portions. Place in shallow pan. Mix orange concentrate, parsley, lemon juice and dill weed with ½ cup water and ¼ teaspoon salt. Pour over fish. Marinate 30 minutes; turn once. Remove fish and reserve marinade. Place fish on well-greased broiler pan and broil 3" from heat for 6 minutes. Turn and broil until fish flakes easily. Baste with reserved marinade. Top with orange slices. Serves 4.

ITALIAN FISH

2-16 oz. pkgs. frozen
  flounder fillets, thawed
1-8 oz. can spaghetti sauce
  with mushrooms

3 T. chopped onion
1 C. mozzarella cheese
  shredded

Preheat oven to 350° F. Arrange fish in a well-greased baking dish. Sprinkle lightly with salt. Mix spaghetti sauce with onion and pour over fish. Bake, uncovered, at 350° F. for 25 to 30 minutes or until fish flakes easily. Sprinkle with cheese and return to oven until cheese melts. Serves 8.

FISH AND TATERS

FISH:
1-1½ lb. frozen block
   haddock or cod
2 T. margarine
½ tsp. salt OR onion salt
¼ tsp. pepper

TATERS:
1¾ C. water
4 T. margarine
¾ tsp. salt
¾ C. skim milk
2¾ C. instant mashed potato
   flakes
6 thin slices onion, optional

(cont.)

68

Preheat oven to 450° F. Place fish on ovenproof platter. Combine margarine with onion salt and pepper and brush on fish. Bake 25 to 35 minutes or until fish flakes easily. Heat water for potatoes combined with 2 tablespoons margarine and salt, and bring to boiling. Remove from heat, add milk, stir in potato flakes, let stand until liquid is absorbed. Spoon into 6 mounds around cooked fish, and top each mound with a slice of onion; drizzle with 2 tablespoons melted margarine. Bake 10 minutes. Serves 6.

LEMON-HADDOCK BAKE

100 calories

2 lbs. frozen haddock fillets
½ tsp. salt
¼ C. chopped onion

¼ C. chopped green pepper
8 lemon slices
¼ C. sauterne
Paprika

Preheat oven to 350° F. Thaw fillets and cut into 8 portions. Place in a greased 7x11" baking dish. Sprinkle fish with salt and top with onion, green pepper, and lemon slices. Pour sauterne over fish and sprinkle with paprika. Cover and bake at 350° F. about 30 minutes or until fish flakes easily. Serves 8.

HERBED MUSHROOM QUICHE

320 calories

1-9" pie crust
¼ lb. Swiss cheese,
    shredded
1 C. lowfat cottage cheese
1 C. skim milk
1-4 oz. can mushrooms, sliced

4 eggs
1 tsp. mustard
½ tsp. thyme leaves
¼ tsp. salt
¼ tsp. pepper

Preheat oven to 425° F. Sprinkle Swiss cheese and mushroom slices over bottom of pie crust. Blend remaining ingredients in blender until smooth. Pour into pie crust. Bake 15 minutes. Reduce oven heat to 325° F. and bake 35 minutes more. Serves 6.

ORANGE-HALIBUT FILLETS

142 calories

1-16 oz. pkg. frozen halibut
   fillets, thawed
3 T. orange juice
   concentrate, thawed

1 T. snipped parsley
1 T. lemon juice
½ tsp. dried dill weed
4 orange slices

Cut fish into 4 portions. Place fillets in a shallow baking dish. Mix concentrate, parsley, lemon juice, dill weed, ½ cup water and ¼ teaspoon salt and pour over fish. Let set to marinate 30 minutes, turning once. Place fish on well-greased broiler pan and broil 3" from heat for 6 minutes. Turn and broil until fish flakes easily. Baste with marinade. Top with orange slices. Serves 4.

SCRAMBLED EGGS AND TOMATOES

136 calories

6 eggs
¼ C. skim milk
½ tsp. salt
¼ tsp. dried oregano

½ tsp. parsley flakes
Dash pepper
1-8 oz. can tomatoes,
    drained and cut-up

Beat together eggs, milk, salt, oregano, parsley flakes and pepper.
Pour into heated non-stick skillet. Cook over low heat lifting gently
to move uncooked egg to bottom. When half done, gently stir in
tomatoes. Finish cooking. Serves 4.

EGG WITH BROCCOLI

110 calories

For each serving;
3 T. cooked broccoli
Garlic salt

1 egg
1½ T. shredded Cheddar
cheese

Coat custard cup with spray-on vegetable coating. Put broccoli in cup and season with garlic salt. Break egg on top of broccoli and top with cheese. Bake 15 to 18 minutes.

CHEESY ASPARAGUS

1 lb. fresh asparagus spears
  or 10 oz. frozen
  asparagus spears

½ C. shredded Swiss cheese
2 T. chopped pimiento
2½ tsp. toasted sesame
  seeds

Cook asparagus in boiling salt water until tender, drain. Mix together cheese, pimiento, and sesame seeds. Sprinkle over asparagus. Heat just until cheese melts. Serves 4.

OMELET WITH VEGETABLE FILLING

325 calories

8 eggs, separated
Water
Salt
Savory leaves
Salad oil
½ lb. mushrooms, thinly
  sliced

1-6 oz. pkg. radishes, thinly
  sliced
2 celery stalks, thinly sliced
1 med. zucchini, thinly sliced
1/8 tsp. pepper
1-8 oz. can tomatoes
1 tsp. cornstarch

Preheat oven to 350° F. Beat egg whites in a large bowl to stiff peaks. In small bowl, beat egg yolks, ¼ cup water, ½ teaspoon salt, and ½ teaspoon savory until thick. Fold egg yolk mixture into egg whites. Cook egg mixture in 2 tablespoons oil in a 12" ovenproof skillet, until eggs are light and fluffy and bottom is brown (about 3 minutes). Place

(cont.)

skillet in oven and bake until top of omelet is golden brown and firm (about 10 minutes). While omelet is baking, cook mushrooms, radishes, celery, zucchini, pepper, ¾ teaspoon salt, and ½ teaspoon savory in 2 tablespoons hot oil, until crisp. Add tomatoes and their liquid, stirring to break up tomatoes. Combine cornstarch and 1 tablespoon water until well blended and stir into vegetable mixture. Cook over medium-high heat until slightly thickened. Loosen side and bottom of omelet and spoon vegetable mixture over half of omelet, and fold other half of omelet over. Slide from skillet onto serving platter. Cover with any remaining vegetable mixture. Serves 4.

MACARONI AND CHEESE PUFF

226 calories

½ C. small elbow macaroni
1½ C. skim milk
1½ C. shredded American
   cheese
3 beaten egg yolks

1 C. soft bread crumbs
¼ C. chopped pimiento
3 T. chopped green onion
3 egg whites
¼ tsp. cream of tartar

Preheat oven to 325° F. Cook macaroni according to package directions. Drain. Combine milk, cheese and ¼ teaspoon salt; cook and stir over low heat until cheese melts. Stir in small amount of cheese mixture into egg yolks and return to cheese mixture and blend well. Stir in macaroni, bread crumbs, onion and pimiento. Beat egg whites with cream of tartar until stiff peaks form. Fold egg whites into macaroni mixture. Pour into 1½-quart souffle dish and bake at 325° F. about 1 hour or until knife inserted in center comes out clean. Serves 6.

BRUSSELS SPROUTS

62 calories

2-8 oz. pkgs. frozen Brussels
   sprouts, partially thawed
1-5 oz. can water chestnuts,
   drained, sliced
1-3 oz. pkg. Neufchatel
   cheese, softened

¼ C. skim milk
¾ tsp. prepared mustard
1½ tsp. lemon juice
1/8 tsp. salt

Cook Brussels sprouts according to package directions. Do not drain.
Add water chestnuts and heat through. Blend cheese and skim milk
and add mustard, lemon juice and salt and beat well. Stir over low
heat just until hot. Drain Brussels sprouts and pour sauce over them.
Serves 8

CRANBERRY BEETS

61 calories

2 tsp. cornstarch
1 ½ tsp. sugar
1/8 tsp. salt
½ C. low-calorie cranberry
  juice

1-16 oz. can sliced beets,
  drained
½ tsp. shredded orange
  peel

Blend together cornstarch, sugar and salt. Stir in cranberry juice and stir over medium heat until thick and bubbly. Add beets and orange peel. Simmer for 10 minutes. Serves 4.

TURNIP-CARROT COMBO

35 calories

1½ C. turnips, peeled &
   cubed
1 T. snipped parsley

1½ tsp. lemon juice
1½ C. sliced carrots
1 T. margarine

Cover and cook turnips and carrots in boiling salt water until tender.
Drain. Add parsley, margarine and lemon juice. Stir together gently.
Serves 6.

BASIL CARROTS

39 calories

6 medium carrots, sliced
1 T. margarine, melted

¼ tsp. salt
½ tsp. basil leaves

Cook carrots in salted water until tender. Combine margarine, salt and basil and toss in with carrots. Serves 6.

VEGETABLE MEDLEY

6 med. zucchini, sliced
2 med. green peppers, cut
  in strips
1 med. onion, sliced
2 cloves garlic
½ tsp. dried thyme or
  oregano

1 lb. mushrooms, sliced
½ C. salad oil
4 med. tomatoes, cut-up
1½ tsp. salt
¼ tsp. pepper

Saute pepper, onion, and garlic until soft. Remove to large bowl. Discard garlic. Saute zucchini and remove. Saute mushrooms. Return all vegetables to pan and add tomatoes. Add seasonings. Cover and simmer until tender.

DILLED BEANS AND CARROTS

89 calories

1 lb. fresh green beans
1 T. dill weed
3 cloves garlic, halved
1 C. vinegar

1 lb. carrots, cut in thin sticks
2 tsp. mustard seed
2½ C. water
½ C. sugar

Snip ends from beans and wash thoroughly. Cook in boiling salt water until almost tender. Cook carrot sticks in boiling water until almost tender. Drain. Combine beans and carrots and add dill weed, mustard seed, and garlic cloves. Combine water, vinegar and sugar and bring to a boil. Pour over beans and carrots. Cool, cover, and chill overnight. Serves 8.

TWICE-BAKED POTATOES

60 calories

3 medium potatoes
⅓ C. hot water
Dash pepper

½ tsp. salt
¼ C. nonfat dry milk powder
Paprika

Scrub potatoes, puncture skins with fork and bake at 425° F. for 1 hour. Cut potatoes in half lengthwise and scoop out insides. Mash potatoes adding water, nonfat dry milk, salt and pepper. Beat until light and fluffy. Replace mashed potatoes gently in potato shell and sprinkle lightly with paprika. Return potatoes to oven for about 10 minutes more. Serves 6.

SKILLET ONIONS

⅓ C. low-calorie Italian
  dressing
3 large onions, sliced
⅓ C. water

2 T. snipped parsley
3 T. shredded Parmesan
  cheese
Paprika

Heat salad dressing with water and ½ teaspoon salt. Place onion slices in a single layer and cover and cook over low heat for 10 minutes. Turn and sprinkle with paprika and parsley and cheese and cook another 5 minutes covered and 5 minutes uncovered. Serves 6.

ORIENTAL SPINACH

25 calories

1-10 oz. pkg. frozen spinach
1-16 oz. can bean sprouts

1-5 oz. can water chestnuts
1 T. soy sauce

Cook spinach according to package directions. Drain and rinse bean sprouts and add to spinach. Drain and slice water chestnuts and stir in. Heat to boiling and drain. Gently mix in soy sauce. Serves 8.

MASHED POTATOES

2 C. shredded cabbage
Instant potatoes (for 4
   servings)

⅓ C. sliced green onion
Dash pepper

Heat 1 cup water and ½ teaspoon salt to boiling. Add cabbage, cover and heat to boiling again. Cook 5 minutes, drain. Prepare instant potatoes according to package directions except: increase salt to ¾ teaspoon, omit butter and use skim milk. Fold in onion, pepper and hot cabbage. Serves 6.

BEAN AND CARROT SALAD

83 calories

1-8 oz. can cut green beans
1-8 oz. can sliced carrots
1-8 oz. can red kidney beans
1 sm. onion, thinly sliced

3 T. chopped celery
2 T. chopped green pepper
1½ T. snipped parsley
¾ C. low-calorie Italian
   dressing

Drain canned vegetables. Mix canned vegetables, onion and celery and place in shallow baking dish. Sprinkle with green pepper and parsley. Top with dressing; cover, and refrigerate several hours before serving. Serves 6.

SQUASH IN A SKILLET

50 calories

2 med. zucchini squash
1 onion, sliced, separated
  in rings
2 tsp. margarine
½ tsp. salt

Dash pepper
1 tomato, cut in wedges
1-2 oz. can sliced mushrooms,
  drained

Clean squash in water and cut off ends. Slice in thin crosswise slices. Melt margarine in skillet and cook onion, salt and pepper until onion is tender. Add squash. Cook covered for 6 minutes, stirring occasionally. Add tomato and mushrooms. Continue to cook until mushrooms and tomato wedges are tender, and squash is beginning to get crisp. Drain off most of liquid before serving. Serves 6.

TOMATO SALAD   35 calories

1 sm. head cauliflower,   1 T. vinegar
  separated   ¾ tsp. seasoned salt
1-16 oz. can tomato wedges,   ¼ tsp. pepper
  drained   6 lettuce cups
⅓ C. chopped onion

Combine all ingredients except lettuce cups; cover and refrigerate
30 minutes. Fill lettuce cups with drained vegetable mixture. Serves 6.

DILLED TOMATO SLICES

33 calories

¼ C. low-calorie Italian
   dressing
¼ C. water
½ tsp. dill weed

½ tsp. salt
1/8 tsp. pepper
1 cucumber, thinly sliced
3 tomatoes, sliced

Combine salad dressing, water, dill weed, salt and pepper. Place cucumber slices in shallow dish and top with dressing. Chill overnight. To serve, top tomato slices with cucumbers and dressing. Serves 6.

CAULIFLOWER SALAD

1 head cauliflower, sliced
¼ C. chopped carrots
¼ C. chopped onion
¼ C. chopped green pepper
¼ C. chopped celery

DRESSING:
½ C. salad oil
½ tsp. sugar
3 T. lemon juice
1 tsp. salt - 1/8 tsp. pepper

Toss all ingredients together and refrigerate 2 to 3 hours.

POLYNESIAN CELERY

45 calories

1 tsp. salad oil
5 C. diced celery
1 can water chestnuts,
    drained & sliced

1 T. chicken bouillon
½ tsp. salt
½ tsp. celery salt

Heat oil in skillet. Stir in all ingredients and cook until celery is crisp-tender, stirring constantly. Serves 5.

BROCCOLI SALAD

2 bunches broccoli
4 cloves garlic
1 T. salt

6 T. olive oil
2 fresh lemons, squeezed

Trim off and discard any tough stalks. Rinse remaining broccoli and stand it in less than ½ pan water. Cover and bring to a boil. Lower heat and cook until it is medium-tender. Drain and cool. Sprinkle with salt. Add cut-up garlic, oil and lemon juice. Mix thoroughly. Serves 6 to 8.

CAULIFLOWER SALAD

1 head cauliflower, chopped
4 green onions, chopped
Mayonnaise

2 medium carrots, shredded
4 stalks celery, diced

Combine the above vegetables and add enough mayonnaise just to moisten the vegetables.

TUNA CARROT SALAD

4 carrots, grated   1 to 2 T. mayonnaise
½ can tuna   Shoestring potatoes, optional

Combine tuna and carrots. Mix with mayonnaise. Serve on lettuce leaf. May be topped with shoestring potatoes. Serves 3.

CABBAGE SALAD

2 lbs. chopped cabbage
1 pt. water
1 T. salt
1 large green pepper
1 shredded carrot

1 C. vinegar
1 T. diced onion
4 tsp. sugar substitute
4 stalks celery, diced

Mix cabbage with water and salt. Let stand 2 hours. Drain well. Add vinegar, onion, sweetener, pepper, celery, and carrot. Mix together.

TUNA CHEF SALAD

78 calories

¾ C. wine vinegar
2 tsp. sugar
2 tsp. dried basil leaves,
   crushed
Dash pepper
8 C. torn lettuce

2 cans water packed tuna,
   drained
1½ C. cherry tomatoes, halved
1 small onion, sliced &
   separated
1 cucumber, sliced
⅓ C. diced celery

Mix first 4 ingredients. Chill. Toss remaining ingredients together.
Pour chilled dressing over and toss lightly. Serves 8.

TOSSED POTATO SALAD

75 calories

½ C. low-calorie Italian
  dressing
2¼ C. hot potatoes, cubed
1 small cucumber, sliced
4 hard-boiled eggs,
  quartered

1 C. diced celery
½ tsp. seasoned salt
1 T. dill weed
3 C. torn lettuce
3 T. snipped parsley

Pour dressing over potatoes, cover and refrigerate 1 hour. Add remaining ingredients and lightly mix together. Serves 8.

TUNA / MACARONI SALAD

1-8 oz. pkg. macaroni
2 T. butter or margarine
2 celery stalks, thinly sliced
2 T. flour
½ tsp. salt

1/8 tsp. pepper
1¼ C. skim milk
2 T. grated Romano cheese
1-6½ oz. can tuna, drained
   & flaked
10 small olives, finely chopped

Prepare macaroni according to package directions. Set aside. Melt butter in 2-quart saucepan. Add celery and cook until tender. Stir in flour, salt and pepper until well blended. Gradually stir in milk and cook until mixture begins to thicken. Stir in cheese and tuna and heat through. Pour mixture over macaroni. Sprinkle with olives. Serves 6.

CHEF SALAD

160 calories

6 C. torn lettuce
2 tomatoes, cut in wedges
4 hard-boiled eggs, sliced
1 onion, sliced
4 oz. cooked ham, sliced

4 oz. shredded Cheddar cheese
1/3 C. low-calorie Italian
   dressing
1/3 C. low-calorie French
   dressing

Gently combine all ingredients except dressings in a salad bowl.
Combine dressing and pour over salad. Toss gently. Serves 8.

BANANA CUSTARD

210 calories

2 C. skim milk
2 eggs
¼ C. sugar

½ tsp. rum extract
¼ C. red currant jelly
1 banana

Combine milk, eggs and sugar in saucepan. Cook over low heat until mixture thickens (do NOT boil), stirring constantly. Stir in extract and spoon custard into 4 dessert dishes. Cover and refrigerate about 1 hour. Before serving, melt jelly and stir in diced banana. Spoon ¼ of jelly mixture on top of each custard. Serves 4.

ASPIC SALAD

65 calories

1 ½ C. tomato juice
1 bay leaf
¼ tsp. celery salt
1/8 tsp. onion salt

1 env. unflavored gelatin
½ C. water
2 T. lemon juice
3 hard-cooked eggs, sliced

Combine 1 cup of tomato juice with bay leaf, celery salt and onion salt and simmer 5 minutes. Remove from heat and discard bay leaf. Soften gelatin in remaining tomato juice and add to hot mixture. Stir in water and lemon juice. Chill until partially set. Pour half of mixture into ring mold. Press egg slices into gelatin and pour remaining mixture over egg slices. Chill until firm. Unmold to serve. Serves 4.

RHUBARB-STRAWBERRY CHILL

56 calories

3 C. fresh rhubarb, sliced
⅓ C. sugar
1 C. water
1 T. cornstarch

¼ C. cold water
1½ tsp. lemon juice
2 drops red food coloring
2 C. fresh strawberries

Combine rhubarb, sugar and 1 cup water and bring to boiling. Reduce heat and simmer until almost tender, about 2 minutes. Remove from heat. Drain, reserving syrup. Add enough water to syrup to make 1¼ cups. Mix in 1 tablespoon cornstarch, salt, and cold water. Cook and stir until thick and bubbly. Cook 2 minutes more. Cool slightly and stir in lemon juice and red food coloring. Gently stir in rhubarb and strawberries. Chill. Serves 8.

SPICED CITRUS FRUIT CUP

1-16 oz. can mixed orange
   and grapefruit sections
2" stick cinnamon

Dash ground cloves
Dash ginger

In saucepan, combine undrained fruit, cinnamon, cloves and ginger.
Simmer 10 minutes. Remove cinnamon and chill, covered. Serves 5.

MARINATED FRUIT

85 calories

1-20 oz. can pineapple
  chunks
1 apple, cored
1 pear, cored
1 nectarine, pitted

3 T. orange juice concentrate,
  thawed
1 T. honey
1 tsp. snipped parsley

Drain pineapple, reserving juice. Cut fruits into chunks. Mix fruits together in a shallow dish. Mix reserved juices with remaining ingredients and pour over fruits. Stir gently. Cover and refrigerate several hours before serving. Stir occasionally. Serves 8.

TAPIOCA-PLUM PUDDING

185 calories

3 T. quick-cooking tapioca
2 C. skim milk
1 egg, separated
1/8 tsp. salt
Sugar

½ tsp. almond extract
1-30 oz. can purple plums,
   drained & pitted
¼ tsp. cinnamon

Combine tapioca, milk, egg yolk, salt and 1 tablespoon sugar in a
2-quart saucepan and let set 5 minutes. Cook over medium heat,
stirring constantly, until mixture is very hot and beginning to thicken.
(DO NOT BOIL.) Remove from heat and stir in extract. Cover and

(cont.)

refrigerate 2 hours. Beat egg whites to soft peak. Gradually beat in 1 tablespoon sugar until egg whites form stiff peaks. Gently fold egg whites into tapioca mixture. Blend plums and cinnamon in blender until smooth. Spoon half of tapioca mixture into parfait or dessert glasses, top with half of plum mixture, repeat. Refrigerate. Serves 5.

CHEESE FRUIT WHIP

125 calories

1 env. low-calorie
  strawberry flavored gelatin
¾ C. lowfat cottage cheese
4½ oz. frozen whipped
  topping, thawed

1 C. honeydew melon balls
1-8 oz. can crushed pineapple
  in unsweetened juice,
  drained
3 T. snipped mint leaves

Sprinkle gelatin on cottage cheese to soften. Stir in and let stand a few minutes. Stir again to dissolve gelatin. Fold in whipped topping and fruits. Cover and refrigerate until time to serve. Divide into 6 dessert dishes. Serves 6.

MOLDED CANTALOUPE BALLS

55 calories

1 C. boiling water
1 env. low-calorie orange
  gelatin
¾ C. unsweetened orange
  juice

1/8 tsp. ginger
1 C. cantaloupe balls
1 C. honeydew melon
  balls

Pour boiling water over gelatin and stir until gelatin is dissolved. Stir in orange juice and ginger. Refrigerate until slightly thickened. Stir in melon balls. Pour into 6 individual molds and refrigerate at least 4 hours. Unmold to serve. Serves 6.

BAKED APPLES

4 red Delicious apples,
   cored
½ C. water

1 tsp. lemon juice
½ tsp. vanilla extract
½ tsp. cinnamon

Pare apples halfway down. Place in shallow casserole. Add water, lemon juice and vanilla. Sprinkle apples with cinnamon. Cover and bake at 400° F. for 20 minutes or until apples are tender.

ORANGE CHIFFON

2-11 oz. cans mandarin
  orange slices
½ C. skim milk
3 eggs, separated

½ tsp. salt
2 env. unflavored gelatin
5 T. sugar
4 oz. whipped topping

Reserve ½ cup orange sections. In blender, combine orange sections
and juice and puree. Set aside. Mix skim milk, egg yolks and salt.
Sprinkle gelatin over mixture. Cook until gelatin is dissolved and
thickens. DO NOT BOIL. Remove from heat. Stir pureed orange
mixture into gelatin mixture. Refrigerate until almost set. Beat egg
whites and sugar to stiff peaks. Gently fold whipped topping and
gelatin mixture into egg whites. Pour into mold. Refrigerate until set.
To serve; unmold and garnish with reserved orange slices. Serves 8.

SNOW APPLES

155 calories

1 large lemon
6 medium apples
1 env. unflavored gelatin
¼ C. water

2 egg whites, room temp.
⅓ C. sugar
½ tsp. vanilla
¼ tsp. salt

Grate peel of lemon; set aside. Cut lemon in half and squeeze juice into saucepan. Cut stem end off of apples about ½" down. Dip cut surfaces in lemon juice. Scoop out inside of apple into saucepan. Discard core and leave shell about 1/8" thick. Brush inside of apple with lemon juice. Wrap apples in plastic wrap and refrigerate. Heat apple pieces and remaining lemon juice to boiling. Reduce heat,

(cont.)

cover and simmer until apples are tender. Stir frequently. Sprinkle gelatin over water and let stand 1 minute. Stir gelatin into apple mixture. Blend apple mixture in blender until smooth. Refrigerate until mounds when dropped from a spoon but is not set. Beat egg whites until soft peaks form. Gradually beat in sugar to stiff peaks. Gently fold together apple mixture, vanilla, salt, half of lemon peel, and egg whites. Spoon into apple shells. Sprinkle with lemon peel. Refrigerate until set. Serves 6.

CHOCOLATE FLUFF

¾ C. nonfat dry milk
⅓ C. sugar
2 T. cornstarch
2 T. cocoa
1 env. unflavored gelatin
1/8 tsp. salt

1½ C. cold water
3 egg yolks, beaten
3 egg whites
1 tsp. vanilla
¼ tsp. cream of tartar
1 C. whipped low-calorie topping

Combine first 6 ingredients in a saucepan and slowly stir in water. Cook and stir until thickened and bubbly. Stir about ¼ cup mixture into egg yolks and return to hot mixture. Cook and stir 1 minute more. Cool until partially thickened. Beat egg whites with vanilla and cream of tartar until stiff peaks are formed. Fold egg white mixture into chocolate mixture. Also fold in whipped topping. Spoon into 10 dessert dishes. Chill until firm. Serves 10.

CHOCOLATE-MARSHMALLOW PARFAITS

147 calories

2 C. reconstituted nonfat
  dry milk
1 pkg. low-calorie chocolate
  pudding mix

1½ C. low-calorie whipped
  topping
15 marshmallows, cut-up

Prepare pudding mix using nonfat dry milk. Cover surface of pudding with waxed paper and cool thoroughly. Fold whipped topping into pudding. Chill. Divide half of pudding mixture among 6 parfait glasses and top with marshmallows. Add remaining pudding. Chill. Serves 6.

RASPBERRY SWIRL

2 env. unflavored gelatin
1-10 oz. pkg. frozen
  raspberries, thawed

1-6 oz. can frozen mixed fruit
  concentrate
1 C. low-calorie sour cream

Soften gelatin in ½ cup cold water and stir over low heat until dissolved. Drain berries and reserve juice. Stir juice, punch concentrate and 1¾ cups water into gelatin. Blend 1 cup gelatin into sour cream, gently. Chill both mixtures until set. Fold berries into plain gelatin mixture. Layer both mixtures into mold. Cut through with a knife to marble. Chill until firm. Serves 9.

BANANA TORTONI

84 calories

2 C. reconstituted nonfat
   dry milk
1 pkg. reg. vanilla pudding
   mix

1 ripe banana, mashed
2 stiffly beaten egg whites
4 maraschino cherries, halved

Prepare pudding following package directions, using nonfat dry milk.
Fold in banana and egg whites. Pour into 8 dessert cups and freeze.
Garnish with maraschino cherry half. Serves 8.

VANILLA TORTE

134 calories

12 graham crackers, finely
  crushed
2 T. margarine, melted
¼ tsp. nutmeg
½ C. sifted powdered sugar
1 env. unflavored gelatin
2 egg whites

½ tsp. grated lemon peel
1 T. lemon juice
½ tsp. vanilla
1 env. low-calorie dessert
  topping mix
1 C. low-calorie sour cream

Combine first 3 ingredients. Press onto the sides and bottom of a springform pan. Chill crust. Combine sugar, gelatin, and a dash of salt. Stir in 1¼ cups cold water. Cook and stir over medium heat until gelatin dissolves. Refrigerate until partially set. Add egg whites, lemon peel, lemon juice and vanilla and beat until very light and fluffy. Chill again until partially set. Prepare topping mix according to package directions and fold into gelatin mixture along with sour cream. Place gently in crust and sprinkle with nutmeg. Chill until set.

CHERRY BAVARIAN CREAM

2-1 lb. cans sour red cherries	1 T. lemon juice
1 env. unflavored gelatin	¼ C. nonfat dry milk
2 tsp. or less sugar substitute	¼ C. ice water

Drain cherries, saving ½ cup liquid. Soften gelatin in ¼ cup liquid. Add sugar substitute. Dissolve over hot water. Chop cherries, add remaining ¼ cup liquid, salt, and lemon juice. Add gelatin and mix well. When mixture begins to thicken, combine dry milk and ice water. Beat until like whipped cream. Fold into gelatin. Pour into 3-cup lightly oiled mold. Chill. Serves 6.

STRAWBERRY PIE

2 env. low-calorie
  strawberry gelatin
1½ T. lemon juice
1-9" graham cracker crust
2 C. strawberries, mashed

2 egg whites
¼ tsp. cream of tartar
1 env. low-calorie dessert
  topping mix

Dissolve gelatin in 2 cups boiling water and stir in lemon juice. Combine ½ cup dissolved gelatin and ½ cup cold water. Chill until partially set and place in bottom of pie crust. Chill until almost firm. Add ½ cup cold water to remaining gelatin. Chill until almost set and fold in strawberries. Beat egg whites sprinkled with cream of tartar to stiff peaks. Prepare dessert topping mix according to package directions. Fold egg whites and ¾ cup whipped topping into gelatin and fruit mixture. Pile atop first layer in crust. Chill until firm. Spoon remaining whipped topping around edge of pie. Serves 8.

CHOCOLATE MINT SNOWCAPS

120 calories

1 env. dessert topping mix
¼ tsp. peppermint extract

1 drop green food coloring
1 box chocolate fudge
   pudding mix

Prepare pudding mix according to package directions using skim milk. Prepare whipped topping according to package directions substituting peppermint for vanilla and using skim milk. Fold ½ cup topping and food coloring together. Combine remaining whipped topping and pudding. Divide pudding into 8 dishes and top with 1 tablespoon colored topping. Freeze up to 2 hours and let set at room temperature 15 minutes before serving. Serves 8.

NO-BAKE CHEESECAKE

125 calories

1 C. skim milk
2 eggs, separated, room
   temperature
1/3 C. sugar
1/4 tsp. salt

2 env. unflavored gelatin
1 large lemon
3 C. creamed cottage cheese
1 tsp. vanilla
1 C. whipped topping

Mix well in saucepan; milk, egg yolks, sugar and salt. Sprinkle gelatin over mixture. Cook over medium-low heat until gelatin is dissolved and mixture is thickened. (DO NOT BOIL.) Grate lemon peel and squeeze 1 tablespoon juice from lemon. Blend cottage cheese in blender until smooth. Stir cottage cheese, vanilla, lemon juice, and

(cont.)

1 teaspoon lemon peel into gelatin mixture. Refrigerate until mixture mounds when dropped from a spoon (about 15 minutes). Beat egg whites until they form stiff peaks. Fold egg whites and whipped topping into gelatin mixture. Spoon into 9" springform pan. Refrigerate until set. To serve; remove the sides of the pan and garnish with lemon peel. Serves 12.

9 INCH PIE CRUST

2 T. skim milk
¼ tsp. fruit flavored
  extract

¼ tsp. vanilla
3 slices white bread, toasted,
  made into crumbs

Combine milk and extracts in bowl. Add crumbs and stir with fork until crumbs are moistened. Press into a 9" pie pan. Bake at 400° F. for 10 to 12 minutes. Cool.

CHERRY TORTE

1 C. prune juice
2 T. cornstarch dissolved in
  2 tsp. water
½ tsp. almond extract

¼ tsp. lemon rind
Dash salt
3 C. unsweetened canned
  cherries
9" pie crust - unbaked

In medium saucepan, combine first 5 ingredients. Cook over medium heat, stirring, until thickened. Add cherries. Pour into pie crust. Bake at 400° F. about 15 minutes. Cool. Serves 6.

LEMON SQUARES

82 calories

2 egg yolks
2 tsp. grated lemon peel
⅓ C. lemon juice
½ C. sugar
Dash salt

2 egg whites
¾ C. nonfat dry milk powder
⅔ C. cold water
4 coconut or vanilla bar
    cookies, crushed

Stir together egg yolks, lemon peel and juice. Add sugar and salt and mix well. Combine egg whites, nonfat dry milk powder and water in a large mixing bowl and beat to stiff peaks. Add egg yolk mixture and beat just until blended. Pour into an 8x8" pan. Top with cookie crumbs. Freeze until firm. Serves 12.

CHEESE PIE

1 lb. cottage cheese
1 C. pineapple tidbits & juice
   (packed in unsweetened
   juice)
1 env. unflavored gelatin

1 egg
5 pkgs. Sweet 'n Low
1 tsp. vanilla
1 tsp. lemon juice
Cinnamon to taste

Preheat oven to 350° F. Mash cottage cheese. Soften gelatin in pineapple juice. Combine all ingredients and pour into a 9" pie plate. Sprinkle top with cinnamon. Bake for 30 minutes. Cool and refrigerate. Serves 5.

APPLESAUCE COOKIES

½ C. flour
1 tsp. cinnamon
½ tsp. soda
¼ tsp. salt
¼ tsp. nutmeg
1/8 tsp. cloves
1/8 tsp. allspice

½ C. rolled oats
½ C. raisins
½ C. unsweetened applesauce
¼ C. shortening, melted
1 egg
1 tsp. vanilla
½ tsp. artificial sweetener

Sift together first 7 ingredients. Stir in oats and raisins. Combine remaining ingredients, blend well and add to dry ingredients. Mix well. Drop by teaspoonfuls onto lightly greased cookie sheet. Bake at 375° for 10 to 12 minutes. Makes 2 dozen cookies.

APPLE-ANGEL FOOD CAKE

105 calories

1 pkg. white angel food
   cake mix
5 med. red cooking apples

¼ C. apple jelly
1/8 tsp. ground cinnamon

Prepare cake according to package directions. Bake in jellyroll pan
30 to 35 minutes. Invert to cool. When cake is cooled, preheat oven
to 400° F. Cut each apple in half and slice thinly. Bake slices 10
minutes, cool 5 minutes. Place apples on cooled cake. Heat jelly and
cinnamon in saucepan and spread over apples on cake. Serves 20.

ESPRESSO SPONGE CAKE

150 calories

6 eggs, separated,
   room temperature
½ tsp. cream of tartar
Sugar
2 C. cake flour
1 C. water

1 T. baking powder
1 T. instant espresso
½ tsp. salt
½ tsp. vanilla
Mocha Frosting

Beat egg whites and cream of tartar until soft peaks form. Sprinkle
½ cup sugar slowly over egg whites, beating to stiff peaks. Set aside.
Preheat oven to 350° F. Beat egg yolks, flour, water, baking powder,
espresso, salt, vanilla, and ½ cup sugar until light and fluffy. Gently

(cont.)

fold egg whites into flour mixture. Pour batter into ungreased tube pan and bake 60 to 65 minutes. Invert cake to cool.

PREPARE FROSTING: ½-3 ounce package whipped topping mix according to package directions, except add 1 teaspoon instant espresso. Frost cake when completely cool. Serves 16.

BANANA BREAD

½ C. shortening, melted
2 T. artificial sweetener
2 eggs, beaten
3 large bananas, mashed
2 T. milk

2 C. flour
1 tsp. soda
1 tsp. baking powder
1 tsp. salt
¼ C. nuts

Mix together in order and bake in a large pan. Bake 45 minutes at 350° F.

CHOCOLATE BROWNIES

1 sq. unsweetened chocolate
⅓ C. shortening
2 T. artificial sweetener
2 tsp. vanilla

2 eggs, beaten
1 C. cake flour
½ tsp. salt
½ tsp. soda

Melt chocolate and shortening in saucepan over low heat. Remove from heat. Add sweetener, vanilla and eggs. Stir until well blended. Add dry ingredients and mix until blended. Pour into greased 8x8" pan. Bake at 350° F. for 20 minutes.

LOW-CALORIE CHOCOLATE CHIP ICE CREAM

2 eggs
1 C. sugar
4 T. flour
Pinch salt
2 sqs. baking chocolate

1-13 oz. can evaporated milk
Skim milk
2 oz. baking chocolate,
 chipped
1 T. vanilla

Mix well: eggs, sugar, flour, salt and chocolate. Scald evaporated milk and pour over egg mixture. Place in double boiler and cook and stir until thickened. Remove from heat. Add enough skim milk to mixture to fill top of double boiler. Then add chipped chocolate and vanilla. Pour into freezer can and add enough milk to almost fill can. Follow freezer directions for freezing. Makes ½ gallon.

LIME SHERBET

70 calories

¾ C. boiling water
1 env. low-calorie lime
  gelatin
½ C. sugar

1½ C. buttermilk
2 tsp. grated lemon peel
3 T. lemon juice

Combine gelatin and sugar in bowl and stir in boiling water until dissolved. Stir in remaining ingredients. Place in freezer until thickened, but not set. Beat until fluffy, pour into freezer tray and freeze until firm. Serves 8.

LIME TOPPING

½ tsp. unflavored gelatin
1 T. sugar
½ C. evaporated skim milk

4 drops green food coloring
1 T. sweetened lime juice

Combine gelatin and sugar and gradually stir in milk. Cook and stir over low heat until gelatin dissolves. Add food coloring. Freeze until very cold and whip to stiff peaks. Makes 2 cups.

CHOCOLATE SAUCE

22 calories/tablespoon

1 oz. sweet cooking
  chocolate
1 T. cornstarch
1¼ C. reconstituted nonfat
  dry milk

1 T. sugar
Dash salt
1 tsp. vanilla
1 tsp. margarine

Melt chocolate in top of double boiler. Blend sugar, cornstarch and salt into a saucepan and slowly stir in milk. Cook until mixture thickens and becomes bubbly. Blend in chocolate. Remove from heat and stir in vanilla and margarine. Stir until margarine melts. Chill. Makes 1 cup.